M000106878

PERSONAL DETAILS

Name	
Address	
Email	
Phone Number	
Fax Number	

LOG BOOK DETAILS

Log Start Date	
Log book Number	

INDEX

PAGE NUMBER	SUBJECT
1	
2	
3	
4	
5	
6	
7	
8	
9	
10	
11	
12	
13	
14	
15	
16	
17	
18	
19	
20	
21	
22	
23	
24	
25	

INDEX

PAGE NUMBER	SUBJECT
26	
27	
28	
29	
30	
31	
32	
33	
34	
35	
36	
37	
38	
39	
40	
41	
42	
43	
44	
45	
46	
47	
48	
49	
50	

INDEX

PAGE NUMBER	SUBJECT
51	
52	
53	
54	
55	
56	
57	
58	
59	
60	
61	
62	
63	
64	
65	
66	
67	
68	
69	
70	
71	
72	
73	
74	
75	

INDEX

PAGE NUMBER	SUBJECT
76	
77	
78	
79	
80	
81	
82	
83	
84	
85	
86	
87	
88	
89	
90	
91	
92	
93	
94	
95	
96	
97	
98	
99	
100	

DEBT TRACKER

Debt:

Creditor:

Payment Dates:

Start Date:

Payoff Date:

Account No:

Starting Balance:

Monthly Payments	Paid
January:	
February:	
March:	
April:	
May:	
June:	
July:	
August:	
September:	
October:	
November:	
December:	
Closing Balance:	

COMMENTS

_____

_____

_____

_____

DEBT TRACKER

Debt:

Creditor:

Payment Dates:

Start Date:

Payoff Date:

Account No:

Starting Balance:

Monthly Payments	Paid
January:	
February:	
March:	
April:	
May:	
June:	
July:	
August:	
September:	
October:	
November:	
December:	
Closing Balance:	

COMMENTS

_____

_____

_____

_____

DEBT TRACKER

Debt:

Creditor:

Payment Dates:

Start Date:

Payoff Date:

Account No:

Starting Balance:

Monthly Payments	Paid
January:	
February:	
March:	
April:	
May:	
June:	
July:	
August:	
September:	
October:	
November:	
December:	
Closing Balance:	

COMMENTS

DEBT TRACKER

Debt: _____

Creditor: _____

Payment Dates: _____

Start Date: _____

Payoff Date: _____

Account No: _____

Starting Balance: _____

Monthly Payments	Paid
January:	
February:	
March:	
April:	
May:	
June:	
July:	
August:	
September:	
October:	
November:	
December:	
Closing Balance:	

COMMENTS

_____

_____

_____

_____

DEBT TRACKER

Debt:

Creditor:

Payment Dates:

Start Date:

Payoff Date:

Account No:

Starting Balance:

Monthly Payments	Paid
January:	
February:	
March:	
April:	
May:	
June:	
July:	
August:	
September:	
October:	
November:	
December:	
Closing Balance:	

COMMENTS

_____

_____

_____

_____

DEBT TRACKER

Debt:

Creditor:

Payment Dates:

Start Date:

Payoff Date:

Account No:

Starting Balance:

Monthly Payments	Paid
January:	
February:	
March:	
April:	
May:	
June:	
July:	
August:	
September:	
October:	
November:	
December:	
Closing Balance:	

COMMENTS

_____

_____

_____

_____

DEBT TRACKER

Debt:

Creditor:

Payment Dates:

Start Date:

Payoff Date:

Account No:

Starting Balance:

Monthly Payments	Paid
January:	
February:	
March:	
April:	
May:	
June:	
July:	
August:	
September:	
October:	
November:	
December:	
Closing Balance:	

COMMENTS

_____

_____

_____

_____

DEBT TRACKER

Debt:

Creditor:

Payment Dates:

Start Date:

Payoff Date:

Account No:

Starting Balance:

Monthly Payments	Paid
January:	
February:	
March:	
April:	
May:	
June:	
July:	
August:	
September:	
October:	
November:	
December:	
Closing Balance:	

COMMENTS

DEBT TRACKER

Debt:

Creditor:

Payment Dates:

Start Date:

Payoff Date:

Account No:

Starting Balance:

Monthly Payments	Paid
January:	
February:	
March:	
April:	
May:	
June:	
July:	
August:	
September:	
October:	
November:	
December:	
Closing Balance:	

COMMENTS

_____

_____

_____

_____

DEBT TRACKER

Debt:

Creditor:

Payment Dates:

Start Date:

Payoff Date:

Account No:

Starting Balance:

Monthly Payments	Paid
January:	
February:	
March:	
April:	
May:	
June:	
July:	
August:	
September:	
October:	
November:	
December:	
Closing Balance:	

COMMENTS

DEBT TRACKER

Debt:

Creditor:

Payment Dates:

Start Date:

Payoff Date:

Account No:

Starting Balance:

Monthly Payments	Paid
January:	
February:	
March:	
April:	
May:	
June:	
July:	
August:	
September:	
October:	
November:	
December:	
Closing Balance:	

COMMENTS

DEBT TRACKER

Debt:

Creditor:

Payment Dates:

Start Date:

Payoff Date:

Account No:

Starting Balance:

Monthly Payments	Paid
January:	
February:	
March:	
April:	
May:	
June:	
July:	
August:	
September:	
October:	
November:	
December:	
Closing Balance:	

COMMENTS

_____

_____

_____

_____

DEBT TRACKER

Debt:

Creditor:

Payment Dates:

Start Date:

Payoff Date:

Account No:

Starting Balance:

Monthly Payments	Paid
January:	
February:	
March:	
April:	
May:	
June:	
July:	
August:	
September:	
October:	
November:	
December:	
Closing Balance:	

COMMENTS

_____

_____

_____

_____

DEBT TRACKER

Debt:

Creditor:

Payment Dates:

Start Date:

Payoff Date:

Account No:

Starting Balance:

Monthly Payments	Paid
January:	
February:	
March:	
April:	
May:	
June:	
July:	
August:	
September:	
October:	
November:	
December:	
Closing Balance:	

COMMENTS

DEBT TRACKER

Debt:

Creditor:

Payment Dates:

Start Date:

Payoff Date:

Account No:

Starting Balance:

Monthly Payments	Paid
January:	
February:	
March:	
April:	
May:	
June:	
July:	
August:	
September:	
October:	
November:	
December:	
Closing Balance:	

COMMENTS

_____

_____

_____

_____

DEBT TRACKER

Debt:

Creditor:

Payment Dates:

Start Date:

Payoff Date:

Account No:

Starting Balance:

Monthly Payments	Paid
January:	
February:	
March:	
April:	
May:	
June:	
July:	
August:	
September:	
October:	
November:	
December:	
Closing Balance:	

COMMENTS

DEBT TRACKER

Debt:

Creditor:

Payment Dates:

Start Date:

Payoff Date:

Account No:

Starting Balance:

Monthly Payments	Paid
January:	
February:	
March:	
April:	
May:	
June:	
July:	
August:	
September:	
October:	
November:	
December:	
Closing Balance:	

COMMENTS

_____

_____

_____

_____

DEBT TRACKER

Debt:

Creditor:

Payment Dates:

Start Date:

Payoff Date:

Account No:

Starting Balance:

Monthly Payments	Paid
January:	
February:	
March:	
April:	
May:	
June:	
July:	
August:	
September:	
October:	
November:	
December:	
Closing Balance:	

COMMENTS

DEBT TRACKER

Debt:

Creditor:

Payment Dates:

Start Date:

Payoff Date:

Account No:

Starting Balance:

Monthly Payments	Paid
January:	
February:	
March:	
April:	
May:	
June:	
July:	
August:	
September:	
October:	
November:	
December:	
Closing Balance:	

COMMENTS

DEBT TRACKER

Debt:

Creditor:

Payment Dates:

Start Date:

Payoff Date:

Account No:

Starting Balance:

Monthly Payments	Paid
January:	
February:	
March:	
April:	
May:	
June:	
July:	
August:	
September:	
October:	
November:	
December:	
Closing Balance:	

COMMENTS

DEBT TRACKER

Debt:

Creditor:

Payment Dates:

Start Date:

Payoff Date:

Account No:

Starting Balance:

Monthly Payments	Paid
January:	
February:	
March:	
April:	
May:	
June:	
July:	
August:	
September:	
October:	
November:	
December:	
Closing Balance:	

COMMENTS

_____

_____

_____

_____

DEBT TRACKER

Debt:

Creditor:

Payment Dates:

Start Date:

Payoff Date:

Account No:

Starting Balance:

Monthly Payments	Paid
January:	
February:	
March:	
April:	
May:	
June:	
July:	
August:	
September:	
October:	
November:	
December:	
Closing Balance:	

COMMENTS

DEBT TRACKER

Debt:

Creditor:

Payment Dates:

Start Date:

Payoff Date:

Account No:

Starting Balance:

Monthly Payments	Paid
January:	
February:	
March:	
April:	
May:	
June:	
July:	
August:	
September:	
October:	
November:	
December:	
Closing Balance:	

COMMENTS

DEBT TRACKER

Debt: _____

Creditor: _____

Payment Dates: _____

Start Date: _____

Payoff Date: _____

Account No: _____

Starting Balance: _____

Monthly Payments	Paid
January:	
February:	
March:	
April:	
May:	
June:	
July:	
August:	
September:	
October:	
November:	
December:	
Closing Balance:	

COMMENTS

_____
_____
_____
_____

DEBT TRACKER

Debt: _____

Creditor: _____

Payment Dates: _____

Start Date: _____

Payoff Date: _____

Account No: _____

Starting Balance: _____

Monthly Payments	Paid
January:	
February:	
March:	
April:	
May:	
June:	
July:	
August:	
September:	
October:	
November:	
December:	
Closing Balance:	

COMMENTS

_____

_____

_____

_____

DEBT TRACKER

Debt:

Creditor:

Payment Dates:

Start Date:

Payoff Date:

Account No:

Starting Balance:

Monthly Payments	Paid
January:	
February:	
March:	
April:	
May:	
June:	
July:	
August:	
September:	
October:	
November:	
December:	
Closing Balance:	

COMMENTS

DEBT TRACKER

Debt:

Creditor:

Payment Dates:

Start Date:

Payoff Date:

Account No:

Starting Balance:

Monthly Payments	Paid
January:	
February:	
March:	
April:	
May:	
June:	
July:	
August:	
September:	
October:	
November:	
December:	
Closing Balance:	

COMMENTS

_____

_____

_____

_____

DEBT TRACKER

Debt:

Creditor:

Payment Dates:

Start Date:

Payoff Date:

Account No:

Starting Balance:

Monthly Payments	Paid
January:	
February:	
March:	
April:	
May:	
June:	
July:	
August:	
September:	
October:	
November:	
December:	
Closing Balance:	

COMMENTS

_____

_____

_____

_____

DEBT TRACKER

Debt:

Creditor:

Payment Dates:

Start Date:

Payoff Date:

Account No:

Starting Balance:

Monthly Payments	Paid
January:	
February:	
March:	
April:	
May:	
June:	
July:	
August:	
September:	
October:	
November:	
December:	
Closing Balance:	

COMMENTS

_____

_____

_____

_____

DEBT TRACKER

Debt:

Creditor:

Payment Dates:

Start Date:

Payoff Date:

Account No:

Starting Balance:

Monthly Payments	Paid
January:	
February:	
March:	
April:	
May:	
June:	
July:	
August:	
September:	
October:	
November:	
December:	
Closing Balance:	

COMMENTS

_____

_____

_____

_____

DEBT TRACKER

Debt:

Creditor:

Payment Dates:

Start Date:

Payoff Date:

Account No:

Starting Balance:

Monthly Payments	Paid
January:	
February:	
March:	
April:	
May:	
June:	
July:	
August:	
September:	
October:	
November:	
December:	
Closing Balance:	

COMMENTS

DEBT TRACKER

Debt:

Creditor:

Payment Dates:

Start Date:

Payoff Date:

Account No:

Starting Balance:

Monthly Payments	Paid
January:	
February:	
March:	
April:	
May:	
June:	
July:	
August:	
September:	
October:	
November:	
December:	
Closing Balance:	

COMMENTS

DEBT TRACKER

Debt:

Creditor:

Payment Dates:

Start Date:

Payoff Date:

Account No:

Starting Balance:

Monthly Payments	Paid
January:	
February:	
March:	
April:	
May:	
June:	
July:	
August:	
September:	
October:	
November:	
December:	
Closing Balance:	

COMMENTS

_____

_____

_____

_____

DEBT TRACKER

Debt:

Creditor:

Payment Dates:

Start Date:

Payoff Date:

Account No:

Starting Balance:

Monthly Payments	Paid
January:	
February:	
March:	
April:	
May:	
June:	
July:	
August:	
September:	
October:	
November:	
December:	
Closing Balance:	

COMMENTS

DEBT TRACKER

Debt:

Creditor:

Payment Dates:

Start Date:

Payoff Date:

Account No:

Starting Balance:

Monthly Payments	Paid
January:	
February:	
March:	
April:	
May:	
June:	
July:	
August:	
September:	
October:	
November:	
December:	
Closing Balance:	

COMMENTS

_____

_____

_____

_____

DEBT TRACKER

Debt:

Creditor:

Payment Dates:

Start Date:

Payoff Date:

Account No:

Starting Balance:

Monthly Payments	Paid
January:	
February:	
March:	
April:	
May:	
June:	
July:	
August:	
September:	
October:	
November:	
December:	
Closing Balance:	

COMMENTS

DEBT TRACKER

Debt:

Creditor:

Payment Dates:

Start Date:

Payoff Date:

Account No:

Starting Balance:

Monthly Payments	Paid
January:	
February:	
March:	
April:	
May:	
June:	
July:	
August:	
September:	
October:	
November:	
December:	
Closing Balance:	

COMMENTS

DEBT TRACKER

Debt:

Creditor:

Payment Dates:

Start Date:

Payoff Date:

Account No:

Starting Balance:

Monthly Payments	Paid
January:	
February:	
March:	
April:	
May:	
June:	
July:	
August:	
September:	
October:	
November:	
December:	
Closing Balance:	

COMMENTS

_____

_____

_____

_____

DEBT TRACKER

Debt:

Creditor:

Payment Dates:

Start Date:

Payoff Date:

Account No:

Starting Balance:

Monthly Payments	Paid
January:	
February:	
March:	
April:	
May:	
June:	
July:	
August:	
September:	
October:	
November:	
December:	
Closing Balance:	

COMMENTS

_____

_____

_____

_____

DEBT TRACKER

Debt:

Creditor:

Payment Dates:

Start Date:

Payoff Date:

Account No:

Starting Balance:

Monthly Payments	Paid
January:	
February:	
March:	
April:	
May:	
June:	
July:	
August:	
September:	
October:	
November:	
December:	
Closing Balance:	

COMMENTS

_____

_____

_____

_____

DEBT TRACKER

Debt:

Creditor:

Payment Dates:

Start Date:

Payoff Date:

Account No:

Starting Balance:

Monthly Payments	Paid
January:	
February:	
March:	
April:	
May:	
June:	
July:	
August:	
September:	
October:	
November:	
December:	
Closing Balance:	

COMMENTS

_____

_____

_____

_____

DEBT TRACKER

Debt:

Creditor:

Payment Dates:

Start Date:

Payoff Date:

Account No:

Starting Balance:

Monthly Payments	Paid
January:	
February:	
March:	
April:	
May:	
June:	
July:	
August:	
September:	
October:	
November:	
December:	
Closing Balance:	

COMMENTS

_____

_____

_____

_____

DEBT TRACKER

Debt:

Creditor:

Payment Dates:

Start Date:

Payoff Date:

Account No:

Starting Balance:

Monthly Payments	Paid
January:	
February:	
March:	
April:	
May:	
June:	
July:	
August:	
September:	
October:	
November:	
December:	
Closing Balance:	

COMMENTS

_____

_____

_____

_____

DEBT TRACKER

Debt:

Creditor:

Payment Dates:

Start Date:

Payoff Date:

Account No:

Starting Balance:

Monthly Payments	Paid
January:	
February:	
March:	
April:	
May:	
June:	
July:	
August:	
September:	
October:	
November:	
December:	
Closing Balance:	

COMMENTS

DEBT TRACKER

Debt:

Creditor:

Payment Dates:

Start Date:

Payoff Date:

Account No:

Starting Balance:

Monthly Payments	Paid
January:	
February:	
March:	
April:	
May:	
June:	
July:	
August:	
September:	
October:	
November:	
December:	
Closing Balance:	

COMMENTS

_____

_____

_____

_____

DEBT TRACKER

Debt:

Creditor:

Payment Dates:

Start Date:

Payoff Date:

Account No:

Starting Balance:

Monthly Payments	Paid
January:	
February:	
March:	
April:	
May:	
June:	
July:	
August:	
September:	
October:	
November:	
December:	
Closing Balance:	

COMMENTS

DEBT TRACKER

Debt:

Creditor:

Payment Dates:

Start Date:

Payoff Date:

Account No:

Starting Balance:

Monthly Payments	Paid
January:	
February:	
March:	
April:	
May:	
June:	
July:	
August:	
September:	
October:	
November:	
December:	
Closing Balance:	

COMMENTS

_____

_____

_____

_____

DEBT TRACKER

Debt:

Creditor:

Payment Dates:

Start Date:

Payoff Date:

Account No:

Starting Balance:

Monthly Payments	Paid
January:	
February:	
March:	
April:	
May:	
June:	
July:	
August:	
September:	
October:	
November:	
December:	
Closing Balance:	

COMMENTS

DEBT TRACKER

Debt:

Creditor:

Payment Dates:

Start Date:

Payoff Date:

Account No:

Starting Balance:

Monthly Payments	Paid
January:	
February:	
March:	
April:	
May:	
June:	
July:	
August:	
September:	
October:	
November:	
December:	
Closing Balance:	

COMMENTS

_____

_____

_____

_____

DEBT TRACKER

Debt:

Creditor:

Payment Dates:

Start Date:

Payoff Date:

Account No:

Starting Balance:

Monthly Payments	Paid
January:	
February:	
March:	
April:	
May:	
June:	
July:	
August:	
September:	
October:	
November:	
December:	
Closing Balance:	

COMMENTS

_____

_____

_____

_____

DEBT TRACKER

Debt:

Creditor:

Payment Dates:

Start Date:

Payoff Date:

Account No:

Starting Balance:

Monthly Payments	Paid
January:	
February:	
March:	
April:	
May:	
June:	
July:	
August:	
September:	
October:	
November:	
December:	
Closing Balance:	

COMMENTS

_____

_____

_____

_____

DEBT TRACKER

Debt:

Creditor:

Payment Dates:

Start Date:

Payoff Date:

Account No:

Starting Balance:

Monthly Payments	Paid
January:	
February:	
March:	
April:	
May:	
June:	
July:	
August:	
September:	
October:	
November:	
December:	
Closing Balance:	

COMMENTS

DEBT TRACKER

Debt:

Creditor:

Payment Dates:

Start Date:

Payoff Date:

Account No:

Starting Balance:

Monthly Payments	Paid
January:	
February:	
March:	
April:	
May:	
June:	
July:	
August:	
September:	
October:	
November:	
December:	
Closing Balance:	

COMMENTS

_____

_____

_____

_____

DEBT TRACKER

Debt:

Creditor:

Payment Dates:

Start Date:

Payoff Date:

Account No:

Starting Balance:

Monthly Payments	Paid
January:	
February:	
March:	
April:	
May:	
June:	
July:	
August:	
September:	
October:	
November:	
December:	
Closing Balance:	

COMMENTS

DEBT TRACKER

Debt:

Creditor:

Payment Dates:

Start Date:

Payoff Date:

Account No:

Starting Balance:

Monthly Payments	Paid
January:	
February:	
March:	
April:	
May:	
June:	
July:	
August:	
September:	
October:	
November:	
December:	
Closing Balance:	

COMMENTS

_____

_____

_____

_____

DEBT TRACKER

Debt: _____

Creditor: _____

Payment Dates: _____

Start Date: _____

Payoff Date: _____

Account No: _____

Starting Balance: _____

Monthly Payments	Paid
January:	
February:	
March:	
April:	
May:	
June:	
July:	
August:	
September:	
October:	
November:	
December:	
Closing Balance:	

COMMENTS

_____

_____

_____

_____

DEBT TRACKER

Debt:

Creditor:

Payment Dates:

Start Date:

Payoff Date:

Account No:

Starting Balance:

Monthly Payments	Paid
January:	
February:	
March:	
April:	
May:	
June:	
July:	
August:	
September:	
October:	
November:	
December:	
Closing Balance:	

COMMENTS

_____

_____

_____

_____

DEBT TRACKER

Debt: _____

Creditor: _____

Payment Dates: _____

Start Date: _____

Payoff Date: _____

Account No: _____

Starting Balance: _____

Monthly Payments	Paid
January:	
February:	
March:	
April:	
May:	
June:	
July:	
August:	
September:	
October:	
November:	
December:	
Closing Balance:	

COMMENTS

_____

_____

_____

_____

DEBT TRACKER

Debt:

Creditor:

Payment Dates:

Start Date:

Payoff Date:

Account No:

Starting Balance:

Monthly Payments	Paid
January:	
February:	
March:	
April:	
May:	
June:	
July:	
August:	
September:	
October:	
November:	
December:	
Closing Balance:	

COMMENTS

_____

_____

_____

_____

DEBT TRACKER

Debt:

Creditor:

Payment Dates:

Start Date:

Payoff Date:

Account No:

Starting Balance:

Monthly Payments	Paid
January:	
February:	
March:	
April:	
May:	
June:	
July:	
August:	
September:	
October:	
November:	
December:	
Closing Balance:	

COMMENTS

DEBT TRACKER

Debt:

Creditor:

Payment Dates:

Start Date:

Payoff Date:

Account No:

Starting Balance:

Monthly Payments	Paid
January:	
February:	
March:	
April:	
May:	
June:	
July:	
August:	
September:	
October:	
November:	
December:	
Closing Balance:	

COMMENTS

_____

_____

_____

_____

DEBT TRACKER

Debt:

Creditor:

Payment Dates:

Start Date:

Payoff Date:

Account No:

Starting Balance:

Monthly Payments	Paid
January:	
February:	
March:	
April:	
May:	
June:	
July:	
August:	
September:	
October:	
November:	
December:	
Closing Balance:	

COMMENTS

DEBT TRACKER

Debt:

Creditor:

Payment Dates:

Start Date:

Payoff Date:

Account No:

Starting Balance:

Monthly Payments	Paid
January:	
February:	
March:	
April:	
May:	
June:	
July:	
August:	
September:	
October:	
November:	
December:	
Closing Balance:	

COMMENTS

DEBT TRACKER

Debt:

Creditor:

Payment Dates:

Start Date:

Payoff Date:

Account No:

Starting Balance:

Monthly Payments	Paid
January:	
February:	
March:	
April:	
May:	
June:	
July:	
August:	
September:	
October:	
November:	
December:	
Closing Balance:	

COMMENTS

_____

_____

_____

_____

DEBT TRACKER

Debt:

Creditor:

Payment Dates:

Start Date:

Payoff Date:

Account No:

Starting Balance:

Monthly Payments	Paid
January:	
February:	
March:	
April:	
May:	
June:	
July:	
August:	
September:	
October:	
November:	
December:	
Closing Balance:	

COMMENTS

_____

_____

_____

_____

DEBT TRACKER

Debt:

Creditor:

Payment Dates:

Start Date:

Payoff Date:

Account No:

Starting Balance:

Monthly Payments	Paid
January:	
February:	
March:	
April:	
May:	
June:	
July:	
August:	
September:	
October:	
November:	
December:	
Closing Balance:	

COMMENTS

DEBT TRACKER

Debt:

Creditor:

Payment Dates:

Start Date:

Payoff Date:

Account No:

Starting Balance:

Monthly Payments	Paid
January:	
February:	
March:	
April:	
May:	
June:	
July:	
August:	
September:	
October:	
November:	
December:	
Closing Balance:	

COMMENTS

_____

_____

_____

_____

DEBT TRACKER

Debt:

Creditor:

Payment Dates:

Start Date:

Payoff Date:

Account No:

Starting Balance:

Monthly Payments	Paid
January:	
February:	
March:	
April:	
May:	
June:	
July:	
August:	
September:	
October:	
November:	
December:	
Closing Balance:	

COMMENTS

DEBT TRACKER

Debt:

Creditor:

Payment Dates:

Start Date:

Payoff Date:

Account No:

Starting Balance:

Monthly Payments	Paid
January:	
February:	
March:	
April:	
May:	
June:	
July:	
August:	
September:	
October:	
November:	
December:	
Closing Balance:	

COMMENTS

_____

_____

_____

_____

DEBT TRACKER

Debt:

Creditor:

Payment Dates:

Start Date:

Payoff Date:

Account No:

Starting Balance:

Monthly Payments	Paid
January:	
February:	
March:	
April:	
May:	
June:	
July:	
August:	
September:	
October:	
November:	
December:	
Closing Balance:	

COMMENTS

_____

_____

_____

_____

DEBT TRACKER

Debt:

Creditor:

Payment Dates:

Start Date:

Payoff Date:

Account No:

Starting Balance:

Monthly Payments	Paid
January:	
February:	
March:	
April:	
May:	
June:	
July:	
August:	
September:	
October:	
November:	
December:	
Closing Balance:	

COMMENTS

DEBT TRACKER

72

Debt:

Creditor:

Payment Dates:

Start Date:

Payoff Date:

Account No:

Starting Balance:

Monthly Payments	Paid
January:	
February:	
March:	
April:	
May:	
June:	
July:	
August:	
September:	
October:	
November:	
December:	
Closing Balance:	

COMMENTS

DEBT TRACKER

Debt:

Creditor:

Payment Dates:

Start Date:

Payoff Date:

Account No:

Starting Balance:

Monthly Payments	Paid
January:	
February:	
March:	
April:	
May:	
June:	
July:	
August:	
September:	
October:	
November:	
December:	
Closing Balance:	

COMMENTS

_____

_____

_____

_____

DEBT TRACKER

Debt:

Creditor:

Payment Dates:

Start Date:

Payoff Date:

Account No:

Starting Balance:

Monthly Payments	Paid
January:	
February:	
March:	
April:	
May:	
June:	
July:	
August:	
September:	
October:	
November:	
December:	
Closing Balance:	

COMMENTS

_____
_____
_____
_____

DEBT TRACKER

Debt:

Creditor:

Payment Dates:

Start Date:

Payoff Date:

Account No:

Starting Balance:

Monthly Payments	Paid
January:	
February:	
March:	
April:	
May:	
June:	
July:	
August:	
September:	
October:	
November:	
December:	
Closing Balance:	

COMMENTS

DEBT TRACKER

Debt:

Creditor:

Payment Dates:

Start Date:

Payoff Date:

Account No:

Starting Balance:

Monthly Payments	Paid
January:	
February:	
March:	
April:	
May:	
June:	
July:	
August:	
September:	
October:	
November:	
December:	
Closing Balance:	

COMMENTS

DEBT TRACKER

Debt:

Creditor:

Payment Dates:

Start Date:

Payoff Date:

Account No:

Starting Balance:

Monthly Payments	Paid
January:	
February:	
March:	
April:	
May:	
June:	
July:	
August:	
September:	
October:	
November:	
December:	
Closing Balance:	

COMMENTS

DEBT TRACKER

Debt:

Creditor:

Payment Dates:

Start Date:

Payoff Date:

Account No:

Starting Balance:

Monthly Payments	Paid
January:	
February:	
March:	
April:	
May:	
June:	
July:	
August:	
September:	
October:	
November:	
December:	
Closing Balance:	

COMMENTS

DEBT TRACKER

Debt:

Creditor:

Payment Dates:

Start Date:

Payoff Date:

Account No:

Starting Balance:

Monthly Payments	Paid
January:	
February:	
March:	
April:	
May:	
June:	
July:	
August:	
September:	
October:	
November:	
December:	
Closing Balance:	

COMMENTS

_____

_____

_____

_____

DEBT TRACKER

Debt:

Creditor:

Payment Dates:

Start Date:

Payoff Date:

Account No:

Starting Balance:

Monthly Payments	Paid
January:	
February:	
March:	
April:	
May:	
June:	
July:	
August:	
September:	
October:	
November:	
December:	
Closing Balance:	

COMMENTS

DEBT TRACKER

Debt:

Creditor:

Payment Dates:

Start Date:

Payoff Date:

Account No:

Starting Balance:

Monthly Payments	Paid
January:	
February:	
March:	
April:	
May:	
June:	
July:	
August:	
September:	
October:	
November:	
December:	
Closing Balance:	

COMMENTS

_____

_____

_____

_____

DEBT TRACKER

Debt:

Creditor:

Payment Dates:

Start Date:

Payoff Date:

Account No:

Starting Balance:

Monthly Payments	Paid
January:	
February:	
March:	
April:	
May:	
June:	
July:	
August:	
September:	
October:	
November:	
December:	
Closing Balance:	

COMMENTS

_____

_____

_____

_____

DEBT TRACKER

Debt:

Creditor:

Payment Dates:

Start Date:

Payoff Date:

Account No:

Starting Balance:

Monthly Payments	Paid
January:	
February:	
March:	
April:	
May:	
June:	
July:	
August:	
September:	
October:	
November:	
December:	
Closing Balance:	

COMMENTS

_____

_____

_____

_____

DEBT TRACKER

Debt:

Creditor:

Payment Dates:

Start Date:

Payoff Date:

Account No:

Starting Balance:

Monthly Payments	Paid
January:	
February:	
March:	
April:	
May:	
June:	
July:	
August:	
September:	
October:	
November:	
December:	
Closing Balance:	

COMMENTS

DEBT TRACKER

Debt:

Creditor:

Payment Dates:

Start Date:

Payoff Date:

Account No:

Starting Balance:

Monthly Payments	Paid
January:	
February:	
March:	
April:	
May:	
June:	
July:	
August:	
September:	
October:	
November:	
December:	
Closing Balance:	

COMMENTS

_____

_____

_____

_____

DEBT TRACKER

Debt:

Creditor:

Payment Dates:

Start Date:

Payoff Date:

Account No:

Starting Balance:

Monthly Payments	Paid
January:	
February:	
March:	
April:	
May:	
June:	
July:	
August:	
September:	
October:	
November:	
December:	
Closing Balance:	

COMMENTS

_____

_____

_____

_____

DEBT TRACKER

Debt:

Creditor:

Payment Dates:

Start Date:

Payoff Date:

Account No:

Starting Balance:

Monthly Payments	Paid
January:	
February:	
March:	
April:	
May:	
June:	
July:	
August:	
September:	
October:	
November:	
December:	
Closing Balance:	

COMMENTS

_____

_____

_____

_____

DEBT TRACKER

Debt:

Creditor:

Payment Dates:

Start Date:

Payoff Date:

Account No:

Starting Balance:

Monthly Payments	Paid
January:	
February:	
March:	
April:	
May:	
June:	
July:	
August:	
September:	
October:	
November:	
December:	
Closing Balance:	

COMMENTS

DEBT TRACKER

Debt:

Creditor:

Payment Dates:

Start Date:

Payoff Date:

Account No:

Starting Balance:

Monthly Payments	Paid
January:	
February:	
March:	
April:	
May:	
June:	
July:	
August:	
September:	
October:	
November:	
December:	
Closing Balance:	

COMMENTS

DEBT TRACKER

Debt:

Creditor:

Payment Dates:

Start Date:

Payoff Date:

Account No:

Starting Balance:

Monthly Payments	Paid
January:	
February:	
March:	
April:	
May:	
June:	
July:	
August:	
September:	
October:	
November:	
December:	
Closing Balance:	

COMMENTS

_____

_____

_____

_____

DEBT TRACKER

Debt:

Creditor:

Payment Dates:

Start Date:

Payoff Date:

Account No:

Starting Balance:

Monthly Payments	Paid
January:	
February:	
March:	
April:	
May:	
June:	
July:	
August:	
September:	
October:	
November:	
December:	
Closing Balance:	

COMMENTS

DEBT TRACKER

Debt:

Creditor:

Payment Dates:

Start Date:

Payoff Date:

Account No:

Starting Balance:

Monthly Payments	Paid
January:	
February:	
March:	
April:	
May:	
June:	
July:	
August:	
September:	
October:	
November:	
December:	
Closing Balance:	

COMMENTS

DEBT TRACKER

Debt:

Creditor:

Payment Dates:

Start Date:

Payoff Date:

Account No:

Starting Balance:

Monthly Payments	Paid
January:	
February:	
March:	
April:	
May:	
June:	
July:	
August:	
September:	
October:	
November:	
December:	
Closing Balance:	

COMMENTS

_____

_____

_____

_____

DEBT TRACKER

Debt:

Creditor:

Payment Dates:

Start Date:

Payoff Date:

Account No:

Starting Balance:

Monthly Payments	Paid
January:	
February:	
March:	
April:	
May:	
June:	
July:	
August:	
September:	
October:	
November:	
December:	
Closing Balance:	

COMMENTS

_____

_____

_____

_____

DEBT TRACKER

Debt:

Creditor:

Payment Dates:

Start Date:

Payoff Date:

Account No:

Starting Balance:

Monthly Payments	Paid
January:	
February:	
March:	
April:	
May:	
June:	
July:	
August:	
September:	
October:	
November:	
December:	
Closing Balance:	

COMMENTS

DEBT TRACKER

Debt:

Creditor:

Payment Dates:

Start Date:

Payoff Date:

Account No:

Starting Balance:

Monthly Payments	Paid
January:	
February:	
March:	
April:	
May:	
June:	
July:	
August:	
September:	
October:	
November:	
December:	
Closing Balance:	

COMMENTS

_____

_____

_____

_____

DEBT TRACKER

Debt:

Creditor:

Payment Dates:

Start Date:

Payoff Date:

Account No:

Starting Balance:

Monthly Payments	Paid
January:	
February:	
March:	
April:	
May:	
June:	
July:	
August:	
September:	
October:	
November:	
December:	
Closing Balance:	

COMMENTS

DEBT TRACKER

Debt:

Creditor:

Payment Dates:

Start Date:

Payoff Date:

Account No:

Starting Balance:

Monthly Payments	Paid
January:	
February:	
March:	
April:	
May:	
June:	
July:	
August:	
September:	
October:	
November:	
December:	
Closing Balance:	

COMMENTS

_____

_____

_____

_____

DEBT TRACKER

Debt:

Creditor:

Payment Dates:

Start Date:

Payoff Date:

Account No:

Starting Balance:

Monthly Payments	Paid
January:	
February:	
March:	
April:	
May:	
June:	
July:	
August:	
September:	
October:	
November:	
December:	
Closing Balance:	

COMMENTS

_____

_____

_____

_____

DEBT TRACKER

Debt:

Creditor:

Payment Dates:

Start Date:

Payoff Date:

Account No:

Starting Balance:

Monthly Payments	Paid
January:	
February:	
March:	
April:	
May:	
June:	
July:	
August:	
September:	
October:	
November:	
December:	
Closing Balance:	

COMMENTS

Date

Date

Date

Date

Date

Date

Date

Date

Date

Date

Made in the USA
Monee, IL
19 May 2020

31432789R00063